ABOUT THE AUTHOR

Charlotte Lunn is a poet, bookseller and workshop facilitator living with chronic illness. After completing her Creative Writing degree at the University of Derby, she became the Events Co-ordinator at Scarthin Books and has regularly reviewed literature for BBC Radio Derby. She is a guest poetry facilitator for Derbyshire Writing School and also offers editing and mentoring services. When she's not writing, you can find her in a pile of snacks, on a yoga mat or part way through a cup of tea.

https://charlottelunn.com/
Twitter: @CharlotteLPoet
Instagram: charlottelunnpoet

Charlotte Lunn
Metamorphosis

Laura,
 Thank you for your support in every sense :)
 I love our beautiful partnership ♡
    Enjoy!
       love,
       Charlotte
        xx

VERVE
POETRY PRESS
BIRMINGHAM

PUBLISHED BY VERVE POETRY PRESS
https://vervepoetrypress.com
mail@vervepoetrypress.com

All rights reserved
© 2021 Charlotte Lunn

The right of Charlotte Lunn to be identified as author of this work has been asserted in accordance with section 77 of the Copyright, Designs and Patents Act 1988.

No part of this work may be reproduced, stored or transmitted in any form or by any means, graphic, electronic, recorded or mechanical, without the prior written permission of the publisher.

FIRST PUBLISHED MAY 2021

Printed and bound in the UK
by ImprintDigital, Exeter

ISBN: 978-1-912565-58-0

Cover image: @alicesayspalace

To you who holds on.
To you who holds onto this book.
Keep going.
You're loved and you're not alone.

CONTENTS

How easy it is to hurt

Little shocks	13
I know what you did	14
Who are you today?	15
Tormented	16
Upbringing	17
Sense of an ending	18
I don't have a tongue	19
The dentist	20
Home time	21
We teach girls shame	22
Consent	23
On valentines	25
The fragility in our lips	27

How do you feel on a scale of 1-10?

Persistence	30
Afternoon tea	31
Call of desperation	32
Don't feed the hollow	33
It was a concise winter	34
Dusk	36
Paranoia: unplugged	38

Sarah	39
Red queen	40
Paranoia: lights	42
Please get comfortable	43
What I should have said	45

A stillness settles - long exhalation

Metamorphosis	48
Semi-detached	50
Sociopath	51
The child that does not exist	52
In search of...	54
Syntax	55
That hovering thing outside your window will help you sleep	56
Making room	59
Vulnerable	58
In my silence	59
Girl	61
I sieve through your truths	62
Wild	63
And then there was you	64
Carousel	66

Acknowledgements

Metamorphosis

How easy it is to hurt

Little shocks

Micro-fibre little
shocks that cause
static to erupt from
skin to skin

how easy it is to hurt
without meaning

I know what you did

the monsters under
my bed have done
less sinister things

than ring-giving to
those possessed -
ornamental, soft

curtains hurting
my eyes into
kaleidoscope sleep

peeping through
to see if it's safe
to leave my room

into boom of
luminous yellow
figures reflected

on kitchen surfaces.

Who are you today?

In front of this mirror,
I am faceless,
different masks hang
on the wall, I

must choose one to
wear for
the rest of the day.

A piece of scalp
and jawbone are
missing from one face,

      another, its mouth
cleaves to the side
an expression unable

to bear much
at all, I choose the
last face, the one
that is perfect,

the one that has not
yet been harmed,
the one that is not

really mine.

Tormented

Walking at a death-like pace in
hell's playground, hands tucked into
sleeves of the little black coat to keep
out acidic veneered words; fur warms
the decaying child.

The devil's creatures chortle.
It rings in the ears of the vexed
decrepit, others walk by - blind
the walking impaired seen as gaseous.

Scapegoat always chosen to be it,
forced to share snacks with them
because they pinky promise to be
your friend, chanting pitilessly

The *pale antique* shatters,
unorthodox their thoughts scream
a reiterate of blows to the head
anguish strengthened by one word

Stupid

Upbringing

You give the
minimum

a contusion of
parental fuses
lost to loving you

in ways you
will never
understand

hands
weren't made to
touch bodies
like this as

bodies form
memories like
sofas that
forget to
forget you

rummaging in
this dark place
for feelings.

Sense of an ending

Our condolences
to the Maid of Honour, her
speech, an epitaph.

I don't have a tongue

    it's used by the one that
    brought me here

        to receive love where
        it did not exist

it hides in mouths that
use it to lie and

    do not know how to kiss

I don't have skin

    it crept away when
    sneered at for its milkiness

        mirrored
        a girl peeling

I don't have hands

    they're contraband for
    knowing how to feel

I don't have lips

    they've kissed thieves, broken
    objects and innocence (see, I don't

        have a tongue for the
        location of my apology)

The dentist

All gums swollen and
dribbling, you would tease me,
my mouth full of metal,

drilling at my *mistakes*. These
vacuumed cheeks like fishbowls,

sugar-free sweets for
the child you *never wanted*. A mouth full of
dreams, fuller than childhood. A blue
distant thing washed down the drain.

Home time

Smothered by
chattering mouths
the body count is
getting loud

until her head is
mine, on shoulders
a spinning top

but when do we
stop?

Wandering hands
in phosphorescent
just down the hall
I feel their

presence. A crack in
the door - this space
has been mocked.

Will you form the
orderly line amongst
the voices till
it's home time?

We teach girls shame

Barely enough breast
to fill a bra but you're 10,
it's time to be a

woman now, buttons
undone two too many to
see a ripple whilst

girls line up to shed
their linings but timing is
what it's all about

because ovulation
is the new black. Did no one
tell you sweetheart? Or

were you too busy tying
your laces?

'We teach girls shame' is a quote from Chimamanda Ngozi
Adichie's *We Should All Be Feminists* (Fourth Estate, 2014)

Consent

You ad lib into
sex because your dick
forgot its lines

I can tell in 30 seconds
that you're not going
to be kind

you've never
made love to a
woman, have you?

You screw with
the idea that sexual
frustration entitles you

into my knickers. Pin
them to your wall or
better yet your floor

shrink wrap them
like the Durex
hiding in your drawers

but whores, are
not only female and
your tail's seen enough

V to be sectioned
so, keep your erection
under wraps and I

don't mean latex but
your tighty whities,
chap.

On valentines

Gynaecology decides
to take a holiday and
postpone your appointment

EVERY
               YEAR

hospital letter reads:

You're not getting any! It's time for your smear

and there's nothing worse
than another woman thinking
she knows your body, just
because she's a woman

I'm sorry but you're not
acquainted with my
cervix and if you were, it
wouldn't let you in for tea,
let alone - male doctor
colposcopies

It's my first time.
My vagina is not a circus act.

Questions asked, your
legs in stirrups:

Where do you live?
Where do you work?
What are you doing today?

I wasn't prepared for
this inquisition, stretched
for spectators in
awkward positions

the meaning of
this screening isn't
to watch me like a movie
but douse me in iodine
swab then release

The fragility in our lips

We stand in an open field
        our attire black, bound by
a white sheet
twisting a small breadth
between -

a smothering.

Words inescapable: no thought can
pass through. We fall to the
ground, the sheet tears and
slips from our faces.

How do you feel on a scale of 1-10?

Persistence

Asking for something over and over
isn't really asking anymore,
is it?

Some jars just don't want to
be opened but
you're here

popping cherries with a
knife

Afternoon tea

Too refined for conversations like
I'm not eating lately

for anorexia to be synonymous
with anxiety. You don't notice the

things we don't talk about yet
you're screaming in the street

Are you making yourself sick?
I mean honestly, who wants to

make themselves sick?
Loss of appetite does not

confirm your diagnosis:

                                      Symptoms
of anxiety:
                               loss of appetite,
overeating,
                       bloating, IBS
        stomach ulcers...

Raising children not to
feel is the reason we're here in

your car, I tell you that
I'm depressed and you say

Well, I already knew that.

Call of desperation

a thrumming heart, beneath
                a silk feathered cage
        a microcosm. valley. in its unhinged bill.
                it faintly hums
                speaking in tongues
                            crooning, cacophonous
                                  in distant fields

                      swooping over hedges
          fanned silk sweeping,   tucking
                it dips - fragile
      a feathered scarf
falls

Don't feed the hollow

Reeling on fish wire
hooked by
cartilage

your flesh lifts from
this body in
one clean swoop, it

gorges on oily fingers
impenetrabilities
scaled resilience

bloating to a
shrivelled prune
it eats to
emptiness

It was a concise winter

sharp   accurate   white,

      like the cut cord doctor that swept you away, covered
in everything you tried so hard to hold onto.

A numbing:
of the new pill they just gave you,
of you can't move until you've finished feeling
'til you've topped up your pot. These leaves leave you with
nothing but bitterness

distrust and loathing of her curves hiding within your arms, as
I was sleeping.
I wish I could be angry because being angry is easier
and I wish you could be angry because every time you talk to
me, I get closer to
replying

because I was too much and not enough and she told me I
didn't need her anymore
after way too many how do you feel today on a scale of 1-10?
you're only allowed to have one problem
at a time

until you laugh
until you cry
all at once.

Dusk

The sky lost its lustre. Grey fell
away like an old
skin   - spinning
ash-curls in
the lake

lucid white
settled in the trees, sifting
between boughs the white engulfs
you until -
        you're forced to the edge

the ground peels and crackles
up the tree veins
filling them like
winter blood

they tear themselves apart,
        become white
you walk into the lake.
There is just you and this mass of water.

White filters through the blue
floating languorously
toward you

you stand in
the centre, ankles immersed
pull back your toe as

the white reaches you.
It latches on

begins to work its way
up your body until you

take your last breath

Paranoia: unplugged

Sweating forehead
Shoulder blades don't fit
Neck won't sit on
The edge of the
Bathtub

Is the plug in?
Or will all the happenings go slipping out?
What clarity was there to be found,
Dear Bathtub, bound
By bubbles?

Is the plug in
Or out?

Sarah

This is not a stay for tea
though you want it
so badly to be
this is not the time to offer
just because she brought you milk

an expectation of kettle simmers as
she moves a little past the door
you stare at everything you know so well and not at all
anymore
she goes to get her bus

a bag full of reminders
lay strewn on the floor

Red queen

as

                                                down
   rabbit   hole
                                                                      watch
no

give

                                                          two
was

                                                                               to
   or   were
                                                                                  more
                  fickle   than
places   for
                             cup   of
            my   head
than   it
                                                                       lick
      your   petals

                                    coat

```
                                          I
            fall
                              the
                         you
                         with
                              hands
                                          to
               just
               faces
    I                                     late
          the                    party
                                 you


               people            changing
                  a                    sweeter
                                 tea
                  gone            quicker
      takes             you                to

      with                  a
          fresh
  of                        paint
```

Paranoia: lights

I'd ask them to leave a
light on but even I know
the real monsters hide
there

left in
the dark

to switch yourself
Off
and
On
and
Off
and
On

Please get comfortable

A witness to this
stranger who speaks
unfamiliar things

but comes from
getting familiar to get
what she wants

hoarding secrets sweetly
your hornet's mouth it
lures or maybe

it's the way you
sound, the way
it likes to purr

all I knew when I
thought I knew you was
you needed sperm

didn't matter where it
came from or if it was to
hurt

cause you didn't need
the friendships, you're
used to being alone

just needed to have a
child, a thing to call
your own, because

it will not know
any better than you.

What I should have said

to the doctor is: try having a panic attack for two weeks instead of sticking a stethoscope down my shirt - without my permission - then tell me I don't feel. Thank God for pills. I don't know how else we'd all keep up with this world. I get where you're coming from, I wouldn't go back to thinking I may die from tripping over my own feet, numb behind the eyes. Sometimes we just need a helping hand along the way. We weren't meant to do this alone. We need people who don't say:*I already knew that, You just got passionate about something so you can't be depressed, People have it so much worse than you, You're too young to be stressed.* We can be happy and sad and lonely and in love and tired and excited just like everyone else.

*A stillness settles -
long exhalation*

Metamorphosis

Year's stump, new birth.
Begrimed footprints
bud in spring,
lidless burettes brimming,
splintered, sticky gum buds:
purge, peel back green,
coated in pale-brown, downy hairs.

Candlelit silhouettes,
fingers grip mucid bark,
these unfledged leaves,
pale brown pores,
gasp.
Forked lightning: up pulled roots.
Sick sycamores, hand in hand:

ring a ring o' roses...we all fall down.

Chestnut leaves fall to disease.
Brittle branches: nutrient sucking soil.
The edge of the forest; treading on
the heels of hail.
Death rakes the leaves.
Befogged torsos, tugged twigs.

Boughs bow to Vivaldi's crescendo:
give a borborygmic groan, green
buds hiding beneath snow. A
log-nipping cold
pimples purplish-black bark:
the frost fleece of bare buckthorns; roots thermal in soil socks.
Timber! years appear; only to begin again.

Semi-detached

There are days when
you can hear me
smile through the
brickwork, unhinged
leaning further
and further into
myself

the doors are open
but I'm not sure I
want you to come in.
There's something
stray about the
connections in the
garden - overbearing
insensitive

language is a
stairway to
impersonation
where the floors
are saving face

blocked by bowels
of underlay.
Feet tread softer.

Sociopath

He had to go to bed with himself
think of all the things he had done

that's why he exploited
the spaces, till there were none

whittling the meniscus of
mistresses, lined up like paper chain ladies

because they've not seen the
creature, that knows so avidly

how to celebrate tears.
An obdurate thing you have been.

What will they write in your eulogy?
Will anyone be there?

The child that does not exist

I apologise for
my uncertainty

sometimes, my body
forgets to bleed
the potential
my womb can exhibit,

I become sceptical as
speculums only
make me more tense

perhaps I'm selfish,
think there's more
to this life than you

maybe you'd be
everything, feed
on all my doubts

but you have to
understand, I'm still
casting it all out,

the sawdust
and the splinters
of human entropy

raised by him
without the self
that lead to therapy

I'm working hard
on being full so
one day if we meet

you'll leave your
home inside me
and land upon
your feet

you'll feel
a Mother's love
the way that it
should be, won't

topple into
strangers whose
hearts don't
know to beat

In search of...

I carry my bones from
home to home like
real people do, to

build cathedrals within
me but Sundays
were never

made for
good people, just
those who want to be,

with all things considered
it may be
too early

for this conversation or
too late

Syntax

The syntax of this
is that you don't
quite fit

anywhere

That hovering thing outside your window will help you sleep

I'd love to sit in a body that doesn't rumble in its wake
that doesn't stir before sleep without the added sweetness
popping candy palpitations

only the stars would understand, you think
one night, shaking in your wrapper skin
as expansive as the solar system

settling within you.

Making room

waves
are homesick for
you to find yourself
when

you feel like
you're drowning
but

you wait in
the place we were
made

naked and
giving too much
your

reasons to reel
them in, are
lost

you're ahead of this
town - heavy with
no

goodbyes, though you
feel it still, midnight trains
will

come with open arms for
your grace

Vulnerable

be frugal with things
and not with feelings

        this isn't skinny living
but fat. It swells

not quite 'tubular
bells' sweltering holy

word to exorcism
but an inner thing

that cares
wants to be shared

quicker than fingers
can cli c k

life experience is
making you sick, you

don't need it to be
sensitive

In my silence

in
  my
    silence

      seedlings shoot up and out behind
rhytidome cellulose, 9-month trunks birthing burls

in
  my
    silence

      copious arms arc over, stretching from their
coppices, intertwining with boughs clustered in copper hands

in
  my
    silence

    irises reminisce when Van Gogh
impressioned them, draping violet velvet contemplates
      roses are irises without eyes

in
  my
    silence

    walnuts shed their milk-skins as aureate azaleas
furbelow, throngs of fuchsia blades smothering slender limbs

in
  my
    silence

        a millennial of eyes pry, mortified
asymmetrical blades alluring aphids; sap suckers, secreting
      sweet honeydew
            tessellated eucalyptus splinters from the thorax

in
  my
    silence

          the ghost flower looms,
i'm caught in hyacinth's grasp, momentarily,
          slipping over buttressed beeches to find my way

Girl

Your dreams are in your stockings
instead of in your hands,
maybe that is why today you
couldn't really stand

the thought of getting glitter
out your sequined pants
once it's there, it's everywhere
it's likely to expand, to get around

much like your heart but
you just need a plan
to borrow stars straight from the sky
and put them in your eyes

remember that you sparkle
to get you through the night.

I sieve through your truths

as you
feign decency, an
obstinate sixty-something

with more ways than years of
solid matter to break
through, Hawking couldn't
have lectured on you.

A conference for my
mind: maker inclined to
project, tumultuous back and
forths when I'm four, streams of

tissues - petrichor. If you
shred my introductions to the
sound of your solipsism they
may sound sweeter. Just a tip

for the next time, you say
they'll eat me alive: get in line
and bring a spoon, binge on your
genes and fill up on you

Wild

If I went nowhere
to devour
wildflowers

I may be a
little harsher
tongued

and
grow
where
you
want
me
gone

And then there was you

I.

When laying here
sheets smelling of your skin
I think how long it would
take to get to you,
the trains aren't running
the streets have gone to sleep
I plan the route
eight hours on my feet,

we meet half way
now in one place
no longer mourning
your morning face
a cavern at your lips,
uprooted hair within my
hands a sleeping disarray
love slowly unravels
in this home, here it is to stay

II.

A stillness settles - long
exhalation, yawns
contagious, we grow our
firsts in this garden

kisses
limbs
will you be mines?
They're all saying *It's nice
to meet you for the first time.*

                Our perfection does not
                make us faultless, just our flaws
                hold us together in a way other
                humans cannot

Carousel

Time moves
forward, heedless
to hiatus

feeding us to
the years, we are
not yet ready for.

These bodies whinny for
overfilled plates, pivot
in tandem, lock fingers

suffocate - tapping on
and off to the splutter
of bridge meets

river. Archways we will
not endure bring us to
places

where our eyes are taken
from us, on the route with

the delicate flowers whose
name I forget, lost
signal grants us a siesta

on the stairs.

ACKNOWLEDGEMENTS

With thanks to those who have previously published my work:

'Tormented', published by the You Will Rise Project, with particular thanks to Paul Richmond for his encouragement and kind words when my writing was in its infancy.

'And Then There Was You', commissioned by Shottle Hall for their Wedding Guide October 2018. Special thanks to James Davis for his continued support throughout the process of writing this poem and my writing career.

'Sarah', published by Impact Magazine Nottingham 09/2019. Thank you, Lauren.

'Girl', published by the Femme Fatales Gals 2020. With particular thanks to Khaya Job. Keep being a powerhouse and doing amazing things!

Thanks also goes to:

My university lecturers and english teachers, for nurturing and inspiring me to be the poet I am today. You're my heroes.

To the Derby and Nottingham poetry community: It took me some time but I finally found my tribe. Thank you for being such friendly and encouraging places to for me to share my work.

To all my writer and poet friends, I'm so lucky to be surrounded by such amazing people who encourage me to go for my dreams. I'm forever in awe of you.

Thank you for editing and offering feedback on this collection before publication as well as being wonderful poets and people: Leanne, Jim, Cullen and Sonia. An extra special thank you goes to Simon who meticulously went through the book with honesty and compassion. You are one of my dearest friends whose talent, resilience and kindness inspires me daily- don't ever change.

To my artist Alice Peake, for your hard work and beautiful cover design. Your art takes my breath away. Let's keep encouraging the odd!

To Sophie Sparham for being your awesome self, offering advice and being the best book launch buddy I could ask for. I've admired you and your work for such a long time and it is an honour to share space with you.

To Stuart at Verve Poetry Press for being one of the loveliest people in publishing, your patience, sound advice and bringing my dream to life. It's been such an honour to work with you on this and I can't thank you enough.

Scarthin Books, the literary hub that has introduced me to cool creatives and customers! My Scarthin family, you beautiful bunch, thank you for your kindness and support, for giving me the best job in the world, the physical space to hold my poetry workshops and the time to grow as a writer.

To Mark, who was my IPT therapist for some time, thank you for believing in me when I didn't. I'm letting the butterflies pass through.

To my beautiful friends for your kindness and support with particular thanks to: Lauren W, Emily, Lauren P, Will, Chloe, Danielle, Adam, Emma L, Meegan, Ella, Nat and Mel.

To Anne, for encouraging me to read from a young age, supporting my writing, for our continued friendship and mutual love of cake.

To the Halls, for welcoming me so whole heartedly into your family. You're all amazing and I'm so lucky to have you.

To Laura, my soul sister, I know you'll resonate with many of these poems and I hope they bring you some solace in your darkest times. You are a gift to this world and you deserve every joy that life has to offer. I'm so lucky to have met you.

To my quirky family with particular thanks to: Robert for taking care of me when I was little and being a friend to me when I needed it the most. You're the best big brother anyone could wish for. To Beki for always treating me like your sister, your years of advice and kindness.

To Mum for being my mother and father, for bringing up 3 children as a single parent, for always listening, for being my biggest fan, for your love. For knowing and understanding everything I've felt in these poems. Through all the adversity you've faced, you've stayed strong but kept your soft edges. For not allowing anyone to douse your beautiful soul. You're incredible and forever an inspiration.

'And Then There Was You' David, the love of my life. Thank you for showing me what love really is and opening me up to new ways of seeing. You move me. Because of you, I am my best self. I love you.

To my younger self for holding on.

ABOUT VERVE POETRY PRESS

Verve Poetry Press is a quite new and already award-winning press that focused initially on meeting a local need in Birmingham - a need for the vibrant poetry scene here in Brum to find a way to present itself to the poetry world via publication. Co-founded by Stuart Bartholomew and Amerah Saleh, it now publishes poets from all corners of the UK - poets that speak to the city's varied and energetic qualities and will contribute to its many poetic stories.

Added to this is a colourful pamphlet series, many featuring poets who have performed at our sister festival - and a poetry show series which captures the magic of longer poetry performance pieces by festival alumni such as Polarbear, Matt Abbott and Genevieve Carver.

Like the festival, we strive to think about poetry in inclusive ways and embrace the multiplicity of approaches towards this glorious art.

In 2019 the press was voted Most Innovative Publisher at the Saboteur Awards, and won the Publisher's Award for Poetry Pamphlets at the Michael Marks Awards.

www.vervepoetrypress.com
@VervePoetryPres
mail@vervepoetrypress.com